Ronda Allott
815-715-8136

W9-AYZ-300

HELP ME — I'M ALONE!

Trusting God in Times of
Loneliness and Grief

by
Joyce Meyer

Harrison House
Tulsa, Oklahoma

Unless otherwise indicated, all Scripture quotations are taken from *The Amplified Bible* (AMP). *The Amplified Bible, Old Testament* copyright © 1965, 1987 by The Zondervan Corporation. *The Amplified New Testament,* copyright © 1954, 1958, 1987 by The Lockman Foundation. Used by permission.

Scriptures marked KJV are taken from the *King James Version* of the Bible.

HELP ME — I'M ALONE!
Trusting God in Times of
Loneliness and Grief
ISBN 1-57794-016-4
Copyright © 1998 by Joyce Meyer
Life In The Word, Inc.
P. O. Box 655
Fenton, Missouri 63026

Published by Harrison House, Inc.
P. O. Box 35035
Tulsa, Oklahoma 74153

Printed in the United States of America. All rights reserved under International Copyright Law. Contents and/or cover may not be reproduced in whole or in part in any form without the express written consent of the Publisher.

Contents

Introduction

A major problem facing people today is grief and loneliness. The two often go together because many people grieve over being lonely.

Loneliness has become even more of a major issue than in the past. In my ministry, an increasing number of people request prayer for guidance and help in handling loneliness.

In His Word, God tells us we are not alone. He wants to deliver, comfort and heal us. But when people encounter painful major losses in their lives, sadly, many never get over them. When tragedy occurs, and the hurt seems unbearable, Satan sees it as an opportunity to attempt to bring an individual or a family into permanent bondage.

The death of a loved one, divorce or the severing of a close relationship can bring grief, and most people go through a grieving process. A key to victory is in understanding the difference between a normal, balanced "grieving process" and a "spirit of grief." One helps the grieving person recover from the loss with the passing of time; the other causes him to grow worse and sink deeper into despair.

I believe one of the reasons why people, especially Christians, become bound by grief and loneliness following a loss is due to a lack of understanding about the "grieving process." Sometimes when God heals, the result is instant. But more often, especially when recovering from a loss, the healing is a process through which the Lord walks His children step-by-step. Obviously, all people do not respond to a loss in the same way or in the same degree, but we all do have emotions that can be wounded and bruised and must be healed.

Jesus came to earth to destroy the works of the devil (1 John 3:8) and to give us abundant life (John 10:10)! If we will learn how to receive what He has made available to us, we will experience that abundant life free from grief and loneliness.

God delivered me from the bondage of grief and loneliness, and I believe He will use the step-by-step process in this book to help you find release, also!

Part 1

Never Forsaken

1

You Are Not Alone

And Jesus came and spake unto them, saying,... lo, I am with you alway, even unto the end of the world....

Matthew 28:18,20 KJV

1

≈

You Are Not Alone

Because he has set his love upon Me, therefore will I deliver him; I will set him on high, because he knows and understands My name [has a personal knowledge of My mercy, love, and kindness — trusts and relies on Me, knowing I will never forsake him, no, never].

He shall call upon Me, and I will answer him; I will be with him in trouble, I will deliver him and honor him.

With long life will I satisfy him and show him My salvation.

Psalm 91:14-16

God wants you to know that you are not alone. Satan wants you to believe you are all alone, but you are not. He wants you to believe that no one understands how you feel, but that is not true.

In addition to God being with you, many believers know how you feel and understand what you are experiencing mentally and emotionally. Psalm 34:19 tells us: "Many evils confront the [consistently] righteous, but the Lord delivers him out of them all." There are many accounts in the Bible of "the afflictions of the righteous" (KJV) and the Lord's deliverance from them.

God Is a Deliverer

God delivered Paul and Silas from prison. (Acts 16:23-26.)

In 1 Samuel 17:37 we read of the Lord delivering David from afflictions. "David said, the Lord Who delivered me out of the paw of the lion and out of the paw of the bear, He will deliver me out of the hand this Philistine. And Saul said to David, Go, and the Lord be with you!"

When you are making progress, Satan often brings affliction to discourage you and will try to make you feel alone. But what Satan intends for our harm, God will work to our good. (See Genesis 50:20.) You can do as David did in the Scripture above and encourage yourself by remembering past victories.

Shadrach, Meshach and Abednego experienced affliction when they remained firm in their commitment to the one true God. (Daniel 3:10-30.) When they refused the command of the wicked king Nebuchadnezzar to worship the golden image he had set up, Nebuchadnezzar cast them into the fiery furnace which he heated seven times hotter than usual!

Nebuchadnezzar was "astounded" (v. 24) to see that Shadrach, Meshach and Abednego met a fourth man in their fiery furnace — One Who was "like the Son of God" (v. 25 KJV). Not only did the three come out of the furnace totally unharmed — they didn't even smell like smoke! (v. 27.)

Verse 30 tells us the king promoted Shadrach, Meshach and Abednego. God will not only bring you out of your afflictions, but He will also bring you up!

Daniel was also afflicted. As punishment for his integrity and commitment to God, Daniel was placed into a lions' den. But Daniel chose to trust in God, and God delivered him by sending an angel to shut the lions' mouths. Daniel came out unharmed! (Daniel 6:3-23.) Keep your trust in God, and you will come out unharmed.

All of these people found that God was faithful. I have also experienced His goodness and faithfulness. I was abused sexually, mentally and emotionally as a child. I have been sick during my life which included ten years of migraine headaches and an attack of cancer as well as several more minor, but nonetheless painful and distressing ailments.

In each case God delivered me and provided answers. But there was a time of waiting on God and being steadfast.

First Peter 5:8,9 states:

> Be well balanced (temperate, sober of mind), be vigilant and cautious at all times; for that enemy of yours, the devil, roams around like a lion roaring [in fierce hunger], seeking someone to seize upon and devour.

> Withstand him; be firm in faith [against his onset – rooted, established, strong, immovable, and determined], knowing that the same (identical) sufferings are appointed to your brotherhood (the whole body of Christians) throughout the world.

As we have seen, afflictions come upon all of us. We all experience a certain amount of grief and loneliness in this life from time to time, but we are not alone. The Bible tells us to resist the devil: "resist" him "stedfast in the faith" (v. 9 KJV). But we can also draw strength from knowing that others know how we feel.

God Is Working for Our Good

God is good, and He is faithful. Several years ago I encountered a major emotional shock that separated me from many people and things very dear to me. God wanted me to move on, but I was not obeying Him. God was working for my good, even though I could not see the good at the time. When I would not move, God moved me and some of the people in my life. I realize now that it was one of the best things that ever happened to me, but at the time I thought my whole world was falling apart. I wasn't sure I would ever recover.

Death and divorce are not the only devastating losses that people face. Losing long-time relationships or a career that has been important to you may be traumatic.

Personal injury preventing you from pursuing a hobby or sport that has been a major part of your life can be very hard emotionally. Actually, losing anyone or anything that is important to us is hard.

My complete recovery took almost three years, but I made steady, definite progress throughout that time. Something that finally helped me be healed of the major pain was an understanding of "soul ties."

"Soul Ties"

Spending a great deal of time with any person or thing leads to a bonding relationship with that person or thing.

As humans, we are spirit, we have a soul and we live in a body. The soul can be thought of as being composed of the mind, the will and the emotions.

Involvement requires mental time, thought and plans. Generally, we talk about what we are most involved in with our mind, our will and our emotions. By giving it a little thought, we can see how involved our "souls" are in the people and things into which we invest most of our time and energy.

If my arm were tied to my side and kept there, immobile, for years, it would have a devastating effect. If it were suddenly untied, I would find it not only withered and weakened, but also disabled. It would be impossible for me to use that arm properly until it had gained back its strength and mobility. I would have to learn new ways to function and to develop the muscles that had atrophied from disuse.

The same thing holds true with our souls. When we have been involved with a person, place or thing for a long period of time, we have developed "soul ties." When that person or place or thing is taken from us, we react as if we were still involved with it. Like an arm that was tied to our side, even though it is later set free, it still "feels" as if it were bound. It does not function properly until some time has passed and some effort has been made to restore it.

Even when we voluntarily walk away from someone or something, our soul may still want to remain where we were. Feelings are very strong, and can cause us much pain and anguish. We must realize that we can use our "will" to decide to do or not to do something. A solid, willful decision will override raging, surging emotions.

There are right and wrong "soul ties." Right ones will balance out in time; wrong ones must be dealt with.

No matter what kind of situation you are dealing with right now, if not handled properly it can cripple you. However, God knows how to handle it!

If you have been injured in an accident, you may have to learn to walk all over again.

If you have lost your spouse to death or divorce, you may have to learn to function as an individual. You may have to learn to do things that you have forgotten how to do or have never done before. You may have to get a job or learn to cook and care for children or make decisions you are not used to making in matters you know nothing about.

If you have lost a job, you may have to learn how to market yourself all over again or even relocate to a new and strange environment.

While you are doing these new things, you may still hurt, but you can take satisfaction in knowing you are moving forward. Each day you are making progress. God promises to be with you in trouble. While you are waiting for Him to deliver you, you can be comforted by knowing He is with you and working on your behalf even though you cannot always see what He is doing in the natural world. Matthew 28:20 says, "...lo, I am with you alway, even unto the end of the world..." (KJV).

2

Loneliness Can Be Cured

...For I will turn their mourning
into joy and will comfort them and
make them rejoice after their sorrow.

Jeremiah 31:13

2

❧

Loneliness Can Be Cured

Loneliness is not a sin. Therefore, if you are lonely, don't add feelings of guilt to your list of wounds.

Loneliness can be cured, no matter what the cause. Some of those who suffer most from loneliness, in itself a form of grief, are the shy or extremely timid; those who feel misunderstood; those in leadership; the divorced and unmarried; the widowed; the elderly; those who feel rejected; those who feel "odd" or different from other people; the abused; those unable to maintain healthy relationships, especially with the opposite sex; those who must relocate or change employment — and the list goes on and on.

There are many causes of loneliness, but many people don't realize they don't need to live with it. They can confront it and deal with it.

The word comes from the root word *lone,* which Webster defines as "without companionship: ISOLATED...located or standing by itself."[1] The adjective forms are *lonely,* meaning "SOLITARY...DESOLATE...dejected by being alone,"[2] and *lonesome,* meaning "dejected, due to a lack of companionship...deserted."[3]

Loneliness often manifests as an inner ache, a vacuum or a craving for affection. Its side effects include feelings of emptiness, uselessness or purposelessness. A more serious side effect of loneliness is often depression, which, in some cases, can eventually lead to suicide.

It is sad to say, but numerous people commit suicide either because they don't know how to handle loneliness or because they don't want to properly face and deal with it in a realistic manner. Even Christians are falling prey to this formidable enemy.

Alone Doesn't Mean Lonely

The dictionary defines the word *alone* as "SOLITARY...with nothing further added... apart from all others."[4] According to Webster, words like, *"Lonely* and *lonesome* convey a sense of isolation felt as a result of a lack of companionship.[4]

Are you alone (independent, solitary, on your own) or are you lonely or lonesome (desolate, deserted, dejected due to a lack of companionship)? There is a difference.

It is very important to realize that just because you are alone does not mean that you must be lonely or lonesome.

Even being in companionship with other people does not guarantee the absence of loneliness.

The conditions that create loneliness are sometimes passing situations. A person who leaves his companions behind and moves to a new home in a new town may experience a temporary feeling of loneliness, but he will eventually make new friends.

But many situations that create a sense of loneliness are much more permanent, and these are the issues that can be dealt with.

While it may not always be possible to keep from being alone, there are always answers to loneliness! *Halelujah!*

Loneliness Caused by Crisis or Trauma

Many times loneliness results from trauma or crisis resulting from the death of a loved one (a spouse, child, parent, close friend or relative), a divorce or separation.

When something happens to make us realize things are never going to be the way they once were, it often creates crisis or trauma in our lives, which can lead to a sense of loneliness and despair.

By its very nature, a crisis situation requires us to go one way or the other, to become better or worse, to overcome or to go under.

We have all seen movies that depict a seriously ill or injured person whose doctor calls in the family and says, "I have done all I can do. The patient has reached a crisis point. What happens now is out of my hands." What the doctor is saying is that within a very short time the person is either going to start getting well or he is going to die.

Crisis always provokes change, and change of this type is hard for everyone involved.

The Process of Grief
Versus the Spirit of Grief

The word *grief* refers to "deep mental anguish, as over a loss: SORROW."[5] To *grieve* is "to feel grief,"[6] that is, to experience mental anguish, to be sorrowful, to mourn, to be distressed.

The grieving *process* is necessary and healthy — mentally, emotionally and even physically. A person who refuses to grieve is often not facing reality, which ultimately has a devastating effect on his entire being.

A *spirit* of grief is another matter entirely. If not resisted, it will take over and destroy the life of the one who has suffered a loss. If not confronted and controlled, it will rob health, strength and vitality — and even life itself.

Let me give you an example.

A friend of mine lost her son to a lengthy battle with leukemia. When the boy died, it was naturally very hard on everyone in the family. They were definitely going through the process of grief, and rightfully so.

However, this friend related to me an incident that exposes the spirit of grief. She said that she was doing laundry one day and began to think about her son, when suddenly she felt something wrap itself around her. It felt gloomy and sad, and she could feel herself almost wanting to "sink" into it.

God gave her discernment that it was a spirit of grief trying to oppress her. She grabbed one of her son's shirts, wrapped it around herself and told the devil that she was using it as a "garment of praise." (Isaiah 61:3 KJV.) Then she began to dance and shout praises to the Lord. As she did so, she felt the oppression leave.

This woman could have opened the door for major long-term problems had she not aggressively confronted and dealt with that oppressive spirit of grief.

Mourning Turned Into Joy

Blessed are they that mourn: for they shall be comforted.

Matthew 5:4 KJV

The Bible makes several references to those who are mourning.

In Jeremiah 31:13, the Lord says through the prophet, "Then will the maidens rejoice in the dance, and the young men and old together. For I will turn their mourning into joy and will comfort them and make them rejoice after their sorrow."

From this verse we see that it is God's will to comfort those who mourn; therefore, we can determine that comfort should come after mourning. If comfort never comes, then something is wrong.

In Isaiah 61:1-3 we read these words of assurance:

> The Spirit of the Lord God is upon me, because the Lord has anointed and qualified me to preach the Gospel of good tidings to the meek, the poor, and afflicted; He has sent me to bind up and heal the broken-hearted, to proclaim liberty to the [physical and spiritual] captives and the opening of the prison and of the eyes to those who are bound.
>
> To proclaim the acceptable year of the Lord [the year of His favor] and

the day of vengeance of our God, to comfort all who mourn,

To grant [consolation and joy] to those who mourn in Zion — to give them an ornament (a garland or diadem) of beauty instead of ashes, the oil of joy instead of mourning, the garment [expressive] of praise instead of a heavy, burdened, and failing spirit....

It is obvious from the principle we see set forth in these Scriptures that God is for complete restoration. He is especially interested in those who are hurting and seeks to restore their joy.

You may be grieving over a loss, but you do not have to stay in that condition the rest of your life. God has promised to turn your mourning into joy. You should hold onto that promise while you are working through the grieving process. Doing so will give you hope for the future.

The Hope Set Before Us

> Hope deferred makes the heart
> sick, but when the desire is fulfilled,
> it is a tree of life.
>
> *Proverbs 13:12*

While grieving over a loss is often necessary and even healthy, care must be taken not
to fall into despair and hopelessness, which
is a heavy burden to bear.

Instead of giving in to hopelessness, heed
the words of David in Psalm 27:13,14:

> [What, what would have become
> of me] had I not believed that I
> would see the Lord's goodness in
> the land of the living!
>
> Wait and hope for and expect the
> Lord; be brave and of good courage
> and let your heart be stout and
> enduring. Yes, wait for and hope for
> and expect the Lord.

No matter what happens in the earth,
there is always hope in God.

In Hebrews 6:17 the Bible states that God has assured us of His will to bless us by backing His promise with an oath, "...so that, by two unchangeable things [His promise and His oath] in which it is impossible for God ever to prove false or deceive us, we who have fled [to Him] for refuge might have mighty indwelling strength and strong encouragement to grasp and hold fast the hope appointed for us and set before [us]" (v. 18).

In verse 19 it goes on to say, "[Now] we have this [hope] as a sure and steadfast anchor of the soul [it cannot slip and it cannot break down under whoever steps out upon it — a hope] that reaches farther and enters into [the very certainty of the Presence] within the veil."

A ship's anchor keeps it from floating away in a storm. Hope does the same thing for our souls. Hope is like an anchor that keeps us on course when we are being tossed to and fro, this way and that, by the storms of life.

You may not understand much when you are hurting and the pain of loss is ripping through your soul, but know and hold on to this one truth: God loves you, and He has a future for you. Hope in Him and trust Him to turn your mourning into joy and to give you beauty for ashes, even as you go through the various stages of grief.

3

Seven Stages of Grief

Lean on, trust in, and be confident in the Lord with all your heart and mind and do not rely on your own insight or understanding.

In all your ways know, recognize, and acknowledge Him, and He will direct and make straight and plain your paths.

Proverbs 3:5,6

3

❧

Seven Stages of Grief

After experiencing a tragedy or loss, almost all of us go through some sort of grieving process. Generally, there are seven basic stages or aspects of this process. Let's look at them individually to try to gain a better understanding of what is happening to us in this process and what we can do to gain the most benefit from it.

Stage 1: Shock and Denial.

These are usually the first things encountered when tragedy or loss occurs. God uses them as protection against complete devastation.

Shock:

A shock is something that jars the mind or emotions with a violent, unexpected blow.

Shock is actually a built-in protection. It gives us time to become gradually adjusted to the change that has taken place. It prevents us from having to face reality all at once.

Before we can press forward, we must have a new mindset. Shock provides us time to develop a new way of thinking about our lives and our futures.

To illustrate, consider an automobile's shock absorbers. They are designed to cushion the vehicle from unexpected bumps in the road. Without them it would fall apart from the violence of the blows it encounters during its travels.

Often we are the same way. We are traveling on the road of life, and most of us are not expecting bumps and potholes. Therefore we are not ready for them when they suddenly show up. Our Holy Ghost-installed "shock absorbers" cushion the blow until we can readjust and adapt our thinking to accommodate the sudden change in the ride.

The stages of shock can last from a few minutes up to several weeks. But if it goes beyond that, something is wrong.

Healthy shock is like a temporary anesthetic; however, we cannot stay permanently under anesthesia. We must move on. Shock is a temporary escape from reality, but if it is not temporary, it can lead to very serious problems.

I recall being with my aunt when my uncle died. He had been sick for quite some time, and even though it was probably inevitable that he would die, my aunt kept saying over and over, "I just can't believe it; I cannot believe he is gone." She was in the initial stage of shock that often comes with a tragic loss.

When going through shock, it is best not to linger in inactivity too long. A woman on my staff experienced a sudden, devastating crisis. I remember her saying, "God told me to keep moving, so I'm going to come to work."

She shared that she was not sure what the quality of her work would be, but she knew it would be disastrous for her if she gave in to the apathy that was seeking to take over and drag her down. In one day, she had lost what seemed to her to be everything of importance to her life. Her general feeling was, "What's the use? Why try to do anything?" She knew that if she was going to survive, she had to counter those feelings with positive action.

When you are going through shock due to a tragic loss, as a believer you must recognize the division between soul and spirit. Even in a time of tragedy or loss you must discern the difference between your human emotions and the true leading of the Holy Spirit.

Denial:

Denial is the refusal to face reality which can often cause emotional and mental illness in varying degrees.

God has equipped us with His Spirit to empower us to face reality, to take His hand, to walk through the dark valleys and to overcome all the obstacles that life brings.

With God's Spirit to dwell within us and to watch over us, we can say with King David, "Yes, though I walk through the [deep, sunless] valley of the shadow of death, I will fear or dread no evil, for You are with me; Your rod [to protect] and Your staff [to guide], they comfort me" (Psalm 23:4).

Even when death brings a shadow over our lives, we can live with hope.

In speaking of hope, think again of Shadrach, Meshach and Abednego in the fiery furnace. (Daniel 3:8-27.) Even though they had to experience being cast into an oven that had been heated seven times hotter than ever before, the Lord was with them in that blazing inferno.

We can look at scriptural accounts such as the one above to encourage ourselves whenever we find ourselves in a tough place. Just as God was with the Hebrew children in that fiery furnace, so that they came out of it loosed and with no permanent damage done to them, so He will be with us in whatever situation we may have to face in life.

It is God's will for us to face reality, to go through and come out victoriously in every way. Facing reality is hard, but running away from reality is even harder.

Stage 2: Anger.

The second stage is marked by anger: anger at God, anger at the devil, anger at self and anger at the person who caused the pain or loss, even if that person died.

Anger at God:

We believe that God is inherently good, and that He is also in control of our lives. Therefore, when tragedy strikes or loss occurs, we don't understand why God does not prevent such things from happening to us and hurting us so badly.

Faced with tragic loss, often we become angry and ask, "If God is good, and all powerful, why does He allow bad things to happen to good people?" This question becomes a major issue when it is we, God's own children, who are the ones suffering.

At such times, reasoning wants to scream out, *"This make no sense at all!"* Over and over the question "Why, God, why?" torments those who are grieving over a loss in their life, just as it also tortures the lonely and the dejected.

In 1 Corinthians 13:12 the apostle Paul indicates there will always be some unanswered questions to deal with in this life:

> For now we are looking in a mirror that gives only a dim (blurred) reflection [of reality as in a riddle or enigma], but then [when perfection comes] we shall see in reality and face to face! Now I know in part (imperfectly), but then I shall

know and understand fully and
clearly, even in the same manner as
I have been fully and clearly known
and understood [by God].

Excessive reasoning, trying to figure out
things for which we will not be able to find
an answer, torments and brings much confusion, but Proverbs 3:5,6 tells us that trust in
the Lord brings assurance and direction:

Lean on, trust in, and be confident
in the Lord with all your heart and
mind and do not rely on your own
insight or understanding.

In all your ways know, recognize,
and acknowledge Him, and He will
direct and make straight and plain
your paths.

When we face a time of crisis in life, we
need direction. These Scriptures tell us that
trusting God is the way to find that direction.

*Trust requires allowing some unanswered
questions to be in your life!*

This truth is hard for us to deal with because human nature wants to understand everything. In Romans 8:6 we are told that "...the mind of the flesh...is sense and reason without the Holy Spirit...."

We want things to make sense, but the Holy Spirit can cause us to have peace in our heart about something that makes no sense at all to our natural mind.

No matter how badly you may be hurting from a loss or tragedy, the Holy Spirit can give you a deep peace that somehow everything will be all right.

Being angry at God is useless because He is the only One Who can help. Only He can bring the lasting comfort and healing that is needed. I encourage you to continue to believe that God is good and to know that whatever has happened does not change that fact. Even when you do not understand your circumstances, continue to believe and say that God is good — because He is!

In Psalm 34:8 the psalmist encourages us, "O taste and see that the Lord [our God] is good! Blessed (happy, fortunate, to be envied) is the man who trusts and takes refuge in Him."

Then in Psalm 86:5 he says of God, "For You, O Lord, are good, and ready to forgive [our trespasses, sending them away, letting them go completely and forever]; and You are abundant in mercy and loving-kindness to all those who call upon You."

Finally, in Psalm 136:1 we are told, "O give thanks to the Lord, for He is good; for His mercy and loving-kindness endure forever."

God is good, but the devil wants us to believe that we cannot trust God and that He does not care for us or love us. If you are having doubts about God's love for you and His faithful care over you, please consider the words of the apostle Paul on this subject as recorded in Romans 8:35-39:

> Who shall ever separate us from
> Christ's love? Shall suffering and

affliction and tribulation? Or calamity and distress? Or persecution or hunger or destitution or peril or sword?

Even as it is written, For Thy sake we are put to death all the day long; we are regarded and counted as sheep for the slaughter.

Yet amid all these things we are more than conquerors and gain a surpassing victory through Him Who loved us.

For I am persuaded beyond doubt (am sure) that neither death nor life, nor angels nor principalities, nor things impending and threatening nor things to come, nor powers,

Nor height nor depth, nor anything else in all creation will be able to separate us from the love of God which is in Christ Jesus our Lord.

Don't be mad at God. Receive the ministry of the Holy Spirit. Listen to the words of Jesus in this passage:

> Do not let your hearts be troubled (distressed, agitated). You believe in and adhere to and trust in and rely on God; believe in and adhere to and trust in and rely also on Me.
>
> And I will ask the Father, and He will give you another Comforter (Counselor, Helper, Intercessor, Advocate, Strengthener, and Standby), that He may remain with you forever.
>
> I will not leave you as orphans [comfortless, desolate, bereaved, forlorn, helpless]; I will come [back] to you.

John 14:1,16,18

Take comfort in those words and resist the devil who will try to convince you to take out your anger and frustration on God.

Anger at the devil:

The Bible says that we should hate evil (Amos 5:15), and since the devil is the source of all evil, then being angry at him can be healthy — if that anger is expressed in a biblical manner.

In Ephesians 6:12 KJV we are told that "...we wrestle not against flesh and blood, but against principalities, against powers, against the rulers of the darkness of this world, against spiritual wickedness in high places." *The Amplified Bible* translation says that we war against "...the world rulers of this present darkness, against the spirit forces of wickedness...."

Our war is definitely not against God or against people, but against the enemy of our souls. How can anger at the devil be effectively expressed? Let me give you an example from my own personal life.

For many years I was mad at Satan because of the fifteen years of child abuse I had endured, but I was venting my anger in the wrong way. I became hard-hearted and harsh in dealing with others. I have since learned that we defeat and overcome evil with good. (Romans 12:21.)

I was angry at the devil because he had stolen my childhood from me, but my acting like him — like the devil — was not repaying him for my loss. Now I am preaching the Gospel, helping people who are hurting, seeing countless lives restored and, in so doing, I am overcoming the evil Satan did to me by my being good to others through bringing the good news of God to them.

This is the way to get back at the devil!

When you have been hurt, the quicker you get involved in helping someone else, the better off you are going to be. Reaching out to other hurting people helps you forget about your own pain.

The only way to repay the devil for hurt and devastation in your own personal life is to aggressively and vehemently do the works of Jesus.

Anger at self:

When tragedy strikes, the question often arises, "Could I have done anything to prevent this from happening?"

A woman I spoke with mentioned that after her husband had died of a sudden heart attack, she kept remembering he had been saying he felt bad. She was blaming herself for not insisting that he see a doctor.

After a tragedy, especially the loss of a loved one, people think of things they wish they had said or done and things they wish they had not said and done.

We can all find plenty to regret in our lives, but regret only produces more agony on top of what we are already experiencing.

Often Satan will take advantage of that situation by placing blame upon us. His tactic is to throw us into a lifetime of guilt, condemnation and self-hatred.

In Philippians 3:13,14 the apostle Paul stated, "...one thing I do [it is my one aspiration]: forgetting what lies behind and straining forward to what lies ahead, I press on toward the goal...."

I like that word "straining." It tells me that, faced with such situations, I may have to "press on" at times, and that there will be opposition from the enemy to overcome.

Endings always bring new beginnings.

Satan strives to keep us out of the new place that God has prepared for us. He wants to trap us in the past and cause us to live in permanent misery. Self-anger and self-blame will do nothing but accomplish the devil's purpose in our lives.

I encourage you to stop tormenting yourself with regret. Satan will always try to attack you when you are in your most weakened state. Guilt, regret and remorse are his favorite weapons. Meditate on the encouraging things, not the discouraging things.

Remember: Don't be angry at God, and don't be angry at yourself. Be angry at the devil, and express that anger in a proper way by overcoming evil with good.

Anger at others:

It is normal to experience anger at anyone who has caused us pain or hurt, even if that person died.

My aunt told me that after my uncle died, she would sometimes beat his pillow at night and yell, "Why did you leave me?" Obviously, her intellect knew that he did not purposely leave her, but her emotions were speaking.

We should learn that emotions have a voice, and when they are wounded, they may react like a wounded animal. Wounded animals can be quite dangerous, and so can wounded emotions if they are followed.

When suffering from a loss, it is important not to let hurt emotions turn into resentment or bitterness. When divorce is the cause of the loss, it is quite tempting to hate the one who caused the separation or even to try to take revenge by hurting back.

Do not waste your life being bitter. Instead, trust God to take whatever has happened and allow it to make you better. The same thing that is hurting you is also hurting multitudes of others. Ask God to take your "ashes" and give you "beauty" for them. Ask Him to allow you to ultimately help others who are working through their grief and loneliness.

Even when a loved one dies, there may be a period of time when you feel angry at that person for leaving you. You may have thoughts such as, "You could have lived if you had just tried harder," or, "How could you leave me to raise the children and face all these heavy responsibilities alone?"

Even though this type of thinking may seem ridiculous to a more stable person in ordinary times, when sudden tragedy strikes and grief sets in, often there is a tendency to "blame" someone else for the pain that is being felt. Thoughts and feelings can be quite erratic, jumping from anger at God, to anger at self, to anger at the devil and then to anger at the person responsible for the loss. This cycle may be repeated many times and even become quite confusing.

Whenever we are hurt, the natural human way to respond is to become angry and to try to defend ourselves against the unbearable pain we are experiencing.

That's why it is so important to understand the grieving process and to be aware of some of the emotions that accompany it. Often in the past we have been taught to place little or no value on our feelings — to disregard them as unimportant.

Just after experiencing a major loss in your life is not the time to deny your feelings or deal with other issues that are anxiety producing or emotionally upsetting. Instead, you must confront your emotions and deal with them.

The answer is not to try to stifle emotions but to recognize them for what they are and to express them in the proper manner.

Stage 3: Uncontrolled Emotions.

People experiencing tragedy often go through various stages of emotions, including sobbing and hysteria. These may come and go when least expected. One minute the person feels that he is going to be all right, then an hour later he finds sadness overwhelming him.

Even those who are normally quite unemotional may experience a great deal of emotion at times of loss. A man who never cries may find himself sobbing uncontrollably at various intervals.

In general, people are afraid of emotions, and an uncontrolled display of emotion may even be fearful.

If you are going through a difficult emotional time right now, I urge you to "fear not" because what you are experiencing at the moment will pass. Good understanding and a lot of help from the Holy Spirit will bring you through the worst of times.

Some people refuse to weep or show any kind of outward emotion, which is not healthy. Pent-up emotions are powerful and need to be released. If you do not release your emotions in times of deep stress, such as the loss of a loved one, those emotions will eat away at you on the inside and may possibly destroy your mental, emotional and even your physical health.

Since God has given us tear glands and an ability to cry, that must mean that there will be times in life when we need to weep.

The Bible makes several references to tears. For example, in Psalm 56:8, the psalmist refers to a bottle in which God keeps his tears. In Revelation 21:4, which speaks of the new heaven and the new earth that will one day be brought forth for God's people, we read that "God will wipe away every tear from their eyes; and death shall be no more, neither shall there be anguish (sorrow and mourning) nor grief nor pain any more, for the old conditions and the former order of things have passed away."

There is healthy weeping and unhealthy weeping. Proper release of wounded emotions is healthy, but beware of self-pity. If left unconfronted, it becomes a monster that will turn you in on yourself in a very unwholesome way.

Compassion is a gift that God has placed within each of us to turn outward toward someone else who is hurting. Compassion turned onto ourselves as pity has a crippling effect.

Self-pity is also addictive. You may think it is a way of ministering to yourself, but actually it is Satan's way of preventing you from moving beyond the tragedy.

You must also beware of using tears to control others. When you are hurting, you need for others to show you love and kindness.

From time to time all of us, no matter how strong and independent we may be, need help from others for a while. But we must remember that although there are times when we need special attention, other people cannot solve our problems. When we look to others, expecting them to make our pain go away, we are making a mistake.

First of all, people cannot give us everything we need. Second, expecting others to meet our personal needs for us places too much pressure on them. It often has a negative effect on our relationships, especially if that dependent behavior is continued for an extended period of time.

It would be quite understandable for a woman who loses her husband to turn to her children to fill the void in her life. This is good to do if, and only if, the woman is truly desiring to "give" herself to her children more now that she has the time and ability to do so. But if the woman's intent is to force the children to assume responsibility for her, they will resent it.

Basically, each person has his own life to live, and no matter how much love there may be between two individuals, no one wants to be controlled or manipulated for selfish reasons.

If you are experiencing pain or hurt right now, I encourage you to trust God and let Him make the adjustments in your relationships that He sees fit to make. He knows that you have different needs now. He knows that void in your life that needs to be filled. When it occurs, God will fill that void in our lives if we wait on Him and refuse to try to use our emotions to control other people.

People don't usually do that intentionally. We may simply be hurting and searching for anything that might alleviate the pain. But

God's way is not to relieve one person's burden
by adding that burden to another person.

Tragedy leaves us in a weakened state,
and Satan will always try to take advantage
of us in our weakest moments. The devil is
not shy about attacking when we are already
down. He sees those lonely, painful times as
golden opportunities to bring us into permanent bondage and misery.

Balance will close the door in Satan's face.

Over the years I have come to realize that
we must learn to work through many things
privately. That does not mean that we don't
need people, because we do. Other people
are definitely used by God to bring comfort
to us when we are hurting. However, if our
"need" for people gets out of balance, it can
block God from working in our life.

My emotions suffered terribly for a number
of years as a result of childhood abuse. During
part of that time I expected my husband to
meet my emotional needs and to fill the void

in my life that had resulted from having the wrong kind of relationship with my father. Certainly the Lord used my husband to help bring emotional wholeness to my life, but I learned that I had to work through most of my problems with God alone.

One of the benefits of having no one to turn to but God is that we get our roots firmly established "in Him." He is the Rock, the solid foundation that never moves. No matter what else around us is shaking, He is always the same.

If you are grieving and lonely due to a tragedy in your life, turn that situation into an opportunity to move into a deeper personal relationship with the Father, Son and Holy Spirit.

Remember: Satan wants to use such times to destroy you, but what he means for your harm, God will work for your good, as you trust Him to do so. (Genesis 50:20; Romans 8:28.)

Stage 4: Depression.

If you are feeling depressed, don't feel bad about yourself. Everyone has experienced depression at some time or another in his life.

When sadness floods the soul, a feeling of depression is quite common, even among those who know and love the Lord. In the Psalms, King David, who was said to be a man after God's own heart, talked about feeling depressed. If such a man of God as King David had to deal with depression, so must each of us.

Temporary periodic depression is just another of the human emotions which everyone experiences during the normal grieving process. But, like the other emotions that come with grieving, depression left unchecked can become a major problem.

The word *depression* refers to a state of being under or an area sunk below normal levels.[7] The simple way to think of it is like this: Jesus is our glory and the *lifter* of our heads. (Psalm 3:3.) But while Jesus lifts us up and puts us over, Satan comes to *drag us down* and to bury us under wounds, hurts and problems.

Depression steals a person's energy. He becomes apathetic and lethargic, desiring to do nothing. If the depressed state continues and becomes strong enough, every movement can become an effort. Depressed people often sleep much more than is really needed — just to avoid life.

Depression can actually become a way of running and hiding in some instances. It can be used to avoid having to deal with life and its problems. **Facing issues is always much more difficult than running from them.**

In my own case I ran from the problems in my life caused by abuse until I was thirty-two years old. When I was filled with the Holy Spirit, one of the first things He started doing in my life was leading me into truth, just as Jesus promised He would do. (John 16:13.) Jesus also said that it is the truth that will make us free (John 8:32), but the truth must be faced if it is to have any positive effect on our lives.

Let's look at the Scriptures to see how King David responded to the age-old problem of depression. In Psalm 42:5-11 he wrote of his sunken emotional state:

> Why are you cast down, O my inner self? And why should you moan over me and be disquieted within me? Hope in God and wait expectantly for Him, for I shall yet praise Him, my Help and my God.
>
> O my God, my life is cast down upon me [and I find the burden more than I can bear]; therefore will I [earnestly] remember You from the land of the Jordan [River] and the [summits of Mount] Hermon, from the little mountain Mizar.

[Roaring] deep calls to [roaring] deep at the thunder of Your water-spouts; all Your breakers and Your rolling waves have gone over me.

Yet the Lord will command His loving-kindness in the daytime, and in the night His song shall be with me, a prayer to the God of my life.

I will say to God my Rock, Why have You forgotten me? Why go I mourning because of the oppression of the enemy?

As with a sword [crushing] in my bones, my enemies taunt and reproach me, while they say contin-ually to me, Where is your God?

Why are you cast down, O my inner self? And why should you moan over me and be disquieted within me? Hope in God and wait expectantly for Him, for I shall yet praise Him, Who is the help of my countenance, and my God.

I love these Scriptures because they show that King David felt depression attacking and flooding his own soul, and yet he resisted it. In other words, although he experienced depression, he would not give in to it. He talked to himself about his situation, and so we must also talk to ourselves during such times.

David remembered the good things on purpose, so that his soul would not be filled with only negative thoughts and influences.

For our own protection, it is vital that we resist long-standing depression. It is impossible to work through the healthy grieving process without experiencing certain feelings of sadness, loss and depression. But once again, my desire is to bring a word of caution concerning an out-of-balance situation that has gone beyond the normal and has crossed over the line into the category of the destructive.

Normal emotions and the proper release of them are healthy. But when emotions are allowed to control us, they can become very destructive. Don't repress your emotions, but don't give them full reign in your life.

Any person who refuses to practice self-restraint, allowing his emotions to get out of control, will ultimately live a life of self-destruction.

Emotions are a gift from God. They are vital to human existence. No one would want to live without feelings. But at the same time, we cannot live our lives by or according to our feelings. For one reason, they are too unstable. We can feel a thousand different ways in the course of a month about the same situation.

People experience this lack of stability in their emotions especially during times of crisis and tragedy, which leads us to the next stage of the normal grieving process.

Stage 5: Waves of Overwhelming Emotion.

When you are going through the grieving process, there will be times when you feel that you have worked through the emotional trauma of your tragedy or loss.

It is perfectly natural to be anxious for all your painful feelings to subside and finally disappear forever. However, that is not usually the way it works. Generally, those moments of subsiding will invariably be followed by surges of seemingly overwhelming emotion.

A good way to think of this emotional ebb-and-flow is to picture the ocean with its mighty waves which beat against the shore with peaceful, smooth intervals between them.

Initially, there seems to be no break in the waves of despair which flow over you and threaten to drag you down. This is a universal feeling which has been common to all people everywhere throughout history. If you recall Psalm 42:6,7 you will remember how David wrote of his despair, "O my God, my life is cast down upon me [and I find the burden more than I can bear]....all Your breakers and Your rolling waves have gone over me."

After some time elapses, however, there begins to be smooth moments between the surging waves. At such moments, you may be tempted to think that the pain may never come back again. Then when you least expect it, there it is again in full force. Something may happen that triggers a memory, and suddenly all the old emotions come back with a vengeance.

The anniversary of the death, loss or separation, and other especially meaningful milestones like holidays and birthdays, are extremely difficult to handle.

I am told that suicide rates rise sharply during holiday seasons. Imagine how hard it is for people to handle the sudden death of a loved one, or any other such tragedy, if they don't know the Lord and His sustaining presence.

Those of us who believe in Jesus Christ receive the comfort of the Holy Spirit, and yet these times are still difficult for us. So we can only imagine what pain must be endured by those who are already empty inside and then suffer the loss of someone or something so meaningful to them.

At such trying times, I am sure that it is easy for Satan to convince them that there is no point in living, that the pain they are experiencing is just too much to bear.

Sometimes I hear people say ahead of time, "I dread the anniversary of that event; I always get so depressed on that day."

Dread is a forerunner of fear, and it never brings a blessing. When I start dreading something, the Holy Spirit always gently reminds me that I am setting myself up for a miserable time.

When you feel yourself beginning to experience feelings of dread, I recommend that you pray and ask the Lord to strengthen you against those overwhelming emotions.

Sometimes we dread things without even realizing we are doing so. Asking for God's help will bring an awareness of what is happening and better equip us to avoid sinking into confusion, disorientation and fear.

Stage 6: Confusion, Disorientation and Fear.

Facing a major change in our lives is one of the most emotionally difficult times that we are called upon to endure. Even if the change was our own choice, it is often hard for us to handle.

If that change comes as a result of tragedy, loss or crisis, then confusion, disorientation and fear are normal. Suddenly our plans for the future have collapsed. A vacation, a home purchase, a company retirement plan that collapses, or other cherished plans are unexpectedly canceled.

It takes time to get new direction. In such moments, many questions come against our minds all at once, and many of them may be pressing for immediate answers.

Even well-meaning friends and relatives may seem to be asking repeatedly, "What are you going to do now? Where will you live? Are you going back to work soon or will you take some time off?"

All of these are valid questions and must eventually be answered.

If you have experienced a sudden life-changing tragedy or loss, you know you need to make some serious decisions about the future. But you may well feel that you are not yet ready to make them!

At such times, your mind is not clear. You may think you have made a decision, and then, suddenly, you change your mind. Your emotions start playing tricks on you; they vacillate back and forth, making decisions even harder than in normal times.

Along with the confusion and disorientation, fear often sets in. You may begin to ask yourself questions like, "What will I do financially? Who will take care of these things I am not used to handling?"

When faced with such troubling questions, I suggest that you meditate on this verse from the book of Hebrews. It always gives me great comfort and hope, and I believe it will encourage you also:

> ...He [God] Himself has said, I will
> not in any way fail you nor give you
> up nor leave you without support. [I
> will] not, [I will] not, [I will] not in
> any degree leave you helpless nor
> forsake nor let [you] down (relax My
> hold on you)! [Assuredly not!]
>
> *Hebrews 13:5*

When we do not know what to do nor what the future holds, it is comforting to know the One Who does know. In Psalm 139:15-17 the psalmist assures us that our heavenly Father does indeed know our past, our present and our future:

> My frame was not hidden from You when I was being formed in secret [and] intricately and curiously wrought [as if embroidered with various colors] in the depths of the earth [a region of darkness and mystery].
>
> Your eyes saw my unformed substance, and in Your book all the days [of my life] were written before ever they took shape, when as yet there was none of them.
>
> How precious and weighty also are Your thoughts to me, O God! How vast is the sum of them!

God is the Alpha and Omega, the beginning and the end. Since this is the case, He is also everything in between. He knows our situation and will lead us and guide us if we trust Him to do so.

Our heavenly Father usually gives us what we need one day at a time. The grace for each day comes with the day. For this reason, it is difficult to look very far into the future and not feel frightened.

As we look ahead, we often feel that we cannot face the difficulties it may bring. But we are looking at them without God's grace upon us.

When we arrive at the place, we will find the grace.

For thousands of years, the Twenty-Third Psalm has ministered comfort to millions of grieving and lonely people. In times of confusion, disorientation and fear, use it as an anchor for your soul:

> The Lord is my Shepherd [to feed, guide, and shield me], I shall not lack.
>
> He makes me lie down in [fresh, tender] green pastures; He leads me beside the still and restful waters.

He refreshes and restores my life (my self); He leads me in the paths of righteousness [uprightness and right standing with Him — not for my earning it, but] for His name's sake.

Yes, though I walk through the [deep, sunless] valley of the shadow of death, I will fear or dread no evil, for You are with me; Your rod [to protect] and Your staff [to guide], they comfort me.

You prepare a table before me in the presence of my enemies. You anoint my head with oil; my [brimming] cup runs over.

Surely or only goodness, mercy, and unfailing love shall follow me all the days of my life, and through the length of my days the house of the Lord [and His presence] shall be my dwelling place.

Psalm 23:1-6

Stage 7: Physical Symptoms.

It often occurs that people who are grieving over a death or other traumatic loss begin
to experience physical symptoms. It seems
almost too much to bear, to feel bad mentally, emotionally and physically.

Emotional upset places tremendous stress
on the physical body. Weaknesses that may
have already been there are often stressed
beyond their limits. Many times the result is
physical pain, sickness or disease.

Various pains in the head, neck, back or
stomach are not uncommon when under
extreme stress. One thing that will relieve
stress is physical exercise.

During periods of grief, often the tendency
is to just sit and "think" (brood). Although
perfectly natural, this tendency must be overcome with forceful, positive action.

If you are going through the grieving
process, I recommend that you at least take

long walks. If you are up to it, I would suggest even more vigorous physical exercise.

Remember: You are already under strain, so don't overdo it.

But it has been proven that exercise does tend to lessen mental, emotional and physical stress and to relax tense muscles.

Loss of appetite, of course, is also quite common when grieving, which is understandable. However, it will be detrimental to your health to discontinue eating for very long. If you are unable to eat very much, try to eat something of good nutritional quality.

Although it may be difficult, also be sure to get the proper amount of sleep. A tired, weak, undernourished and overstressed body is an open invitation to sickness and disease. That's why it is important to get as much physical exercise, nourishment and rest as possible to help the mind and body remain healthy during these stressful times.

I believe that it is also important when grieving and lonely to realize that the things you feel and the various stages of grief you are experiencing are all quite normal and must be gone through in order to return to healthy emotional soundness.

As we have noted, repressed feelings and emotions are very hard on the system. If they are not properly expressed, they can do quite a lot of damage.

Remember: When negative emotions are repressed, they will ultimately come out another way.

Often we think we are hiding things within, but they come out in our attitude or conversation, and even in our physical bodies.

In dealing with all these seven stages of the grieving process, the key word is *balance.*

4

Recovering From Tragedy and Loss

The Spirit of the Lord [is] upon Me, because He has anointed Me [the Anointed One, the Messiah] to preach the good news (the Gospel) to the poor; He has sent Me to announce release to the captives and recovery of sight to the blind, to send forth as delivered those who are oppressed [who are downtrodden, bruised, crushed, and broken down by calamity].

Luke 4:18

4

_~_

Recovering
From Tragedy and Loss

Whatever has happened to cause you to suffer grief and loneliness, you can be sure of one thing: You will be led by the Lord in your recovery. He will definitely let you know when you are becoming excessive or getting out of balance — if you are willing to listen to His Spirit.

It is impossible to set a certain amount of time that it will take to work through the grieving process. That varies with each individual person and situation. But, however long it may be, there will eventually come a time when the Lord will say, *"It is time now to get up and go on. You must let go of the past and finish the course that I have laid out for your life. I will never leave you nor*

forsake you, so be bold, be strong, be coura-
geous, and go forward!"

Each Case Is Different

Generally, the first six months of the
grieving process will be the most difficult. It
could be a little longer or a little shorter
depending on the circumstances. There are
many factors involved that are unique to
each situation:

1. The suddenness of the loss. If a person is
sick for an extended period of time, the
family has longer to become mentally and
emotionally prepared for the death of their
loved one. If the loss is sudden or unexpected, the loss may be more traumatic and
thus more difficult to adjust to.

2. The presence or absence of support mem-
bers. If a husband or wife dies, for instance,
it makes a difference if there are children left
to comfort the surviving parent. If a child is

lost, other children may help to fill the void left in the home by the child's passing.

3. The quality of the relationship between the bereaved and the lost loved one. If the relationship was a strong, loving one, the grieving process will be longer and more difficult than if the relationship had not been as fulfilling.

4. The personality of the survivor. This is especially true in the death of a spouse. Some people are more dependent than others and it takes a greater effort for them to assume the lead role and proceed with life.

5. The depth of the relationship between the grieving person and the Lord Jesus Christ. This is a *major* factor. Tragedy or loss often provokes people to seek a relationship with the Lord, which, of course, brings comfort. But the person who already knows Him "and the power of his resurrection" (Philippians 3:10 KJV) will usually recover much quicker than one who has had no prior personal

As this woman continued in her walk with God, the Lord gave her a special prayer assignment for her husband, warning her that if he did not submit to His (God's) dealings, within six months he would be dead.

The woman prayed, and still the man resisted the dealings of the Lord. Through disobedience, he opened a door for Satan to shorten his life. As a result, the man died of a sudden heart attack.

Although the loss was hard on the wife, it was not nearly as hard as it might have been for someone who had enjoyed a wonderful relationship with her husband. God had warned her, which had prepared her ahead of time.

I noticed that her recovery time was amazingly short. There were issues in her life that had to be dealt with — financial matters and so forth — but overall within a relatively short period of time she was able to adjust and to go on with her life.

The second case:

This one involved my aunt. She and my uncle had known one another in childhood and were married when she was fifteen and he only a few years older. She had never had another boyfriend, nor even dated anyone else.

The two of them were never able to have children, so they were especially close. They worked together in the same bakery for more than thirty years. They did everything together, serving God as partners in the work of the Lord.

They both had experienced a lot of sickness in their lives and had spent a great deal of time caring for each other. Sometimes, the more people have to do for one another, the more they mean to each other.

These two were *deeply* involved in each other's lives. They fit together like a hand in a glove. They had such fun together: fishing, cooking, going to church, etc.

Even though he had been sick for many years, when my uncle died his loss was extremely difficult for my aunt. At the time she was crippled with arthritis in her knees, but could not have the usually prescribed knee replacement surgery because of a heart condition. Therefore, she was more or less housebound for several years after my uncle's death, which only increased her trauma.

Due to these extenuating circumstances, her recovery time actually took years.

Grieving Is Normal, Living in Grief Is Not

From these two cases, we can readily see how the same type of event can affect different people in different ways. Although it is impossible to make an exact prediction of how long the grieving process will last, progress should be seen regularly throughout it.

This progress may be gradual and difficult to perceive at first, but it *definitely* should be seen.

Like a wound healing, the pain may be felt a long time, but complete recovery requires daily improvement. When a physical wound refuses to heal, it is an indication that there is an infection that must be dealt with. I believe the same is true of emotional wounds.

The emotional part of us should heal just like the physical part of us. God gave us emotions just as He gave us physical bodies. He has provided for our emotional restoration in Jesus Christ, just as He has provided for our physical healing in Him. Both of these are our right as believers.

Don't believe the lies of Satan. He will try to tell you that you will never get over the hurt, never be whole again emotionally. While it is true that you may always miss the person or the thing lost, that does not mean that you must suffer permanent grief and loneliness.

Given proper time, grief should dissipate, and you should be able to make a transition to a new season of life. If this transition does not occur within a reasonable time frame, it is an indication that there is a problem somewhere: an improper mental attitude, refusal to face reality or perhaps the presence of abnormal and unreasonable fear.

Whatever the root of the problem, God will reveal it to you if you will spend time reading His Word and seeking Him through prayer and meditation.

Just keep in mind that grieving is normal, but living with a spirit of grief is not.

Overcoming Grief and Loneliness

I would like to share with you two vital points to help you overcome grief and loneliness and gain complete emotional recovery:

1. Know that God is with you all the time.

In Matthew 28:20 KJV Jesus said, "I am with you alway, even unto the end of the world." Then in Hebrews 13:5 KJV we read that God has promised, "I will never leave thee, nor forsake thee."

Grief and loneliness often lead to fear, which in turn provokes all kinds of unanswerable questions such as: "What if I get sick and can't work; who is going to provide for me?" "What if I am alone for the rest of my life?" "What if this pain I am feeling never goes away?" "What if a problem arises that I don't know how to handle on my own?"

"What if...what if...what if..." The questions go on and on, endlessly.

You cannot answer all the "what ifs" in life. But as long as you know that Jesus is with you, you can be assured that He has all the answers you need.

Consider these Scripture passages and let them bring comfort to you:

A father of the fatherless and a
judge and protector of the widows is
God in His holy habitation.

God places the solitary in families and gives the desolate a home in which to dwell; He leads the prisoners out to prosperity; but the rebellious dwell in a parched land.

Psalm 68:5,6

Although my father and my mother have forsaken me, yet the Lord will take me up [adopt me as His child].

Psalm 27:10

Fear not, for you shall not be ashamed; neither be confounded and depressed, for you shall not be put to shame. For you shall forget the shame of your youth, and you shall not [seriously] remember the reproach of your widowhood any more.

For your Maker is your Husband — the Lord of hosts is His name — and the Holy One of Israel is your

Redeemer; the God of the whole earth
He is called.

Isaiah 54:4,5

He was despised and rejected and
forsaken by men, a Man of sorrows
and pains, and acquainted with grief
and sickness; and like One from
Whom men hide their faces He was
despised, and we did not appreciate
His worth or have any esteem for Him.

Surely He has borne our griefs
(sicknesses, weaknesses, and dis-
tresses) and carried our sorrows and
pains [of punishment], yet we [igno-
rantly] considered Him stricken,
smitten, and afflicted by God [as if
with leprosy].

But He was wounded for our
transgressions, He was bruised for
our guilt and iniquities; the chastise-
ment [needful to obtain] peace and
well-being for us was upon Him,

and with the stripes [that wounded]
Him we are healed and made whole.

Isaiah 53:3-5

Sickness also brings grief and loneliness. When we are hurting and pain is flooding our body, we want someone to understand how bad we are feeling. Even though our family and friends may do the best they can for us, we can still find ourselves lonely in our suffering.

Extended illness is even worse because after a while we find that others don't want to continually hear how bad we are feeling. Not only does it not edify them, but it does not help our progress to keep talking about how miserable we are.

When you are sick, you will have the same kind of questions that you have when you are experiencing a tragedy or loss: "What if I never get well; who will take care of me?" "What if I can never do the things that I used to do?" "What if I am never able to go back to work; who will provide for me and my family?" "What if I have to live with this pain for the rest of my life?"

In sickness, you have to apply the same principle that we have discussed in our consideration of grief and loneliness. You have to know that God is your Healer and believe that His power is at work in your body to heal and restore you.

Remember that, "Death is swallowed up in victory" (1 Corinthians 15:54 KJV) and that God has said, "I am the Lord Who heals you" (Exodus 15:26).

Spend a great deal of time with the Lord and allow His resurrection life that is in you as a believer to minister to your physical needs. As you do so, meditate on these Scripture passages:

> ...The everlasting God, the Lord,
> the Creator of the ends of the earth,
> does not faint or grow weary; there is
> no searching of His understanding.

He gives power to the faint and weary, and to him who has no might He increases strength [causing it to multiply and making it to abound].

Even youths shall faint and be weary, and [selected] young men shall feebly stumble and fall exhausted;

But those who wait for the Lord [who expect, look for, and hope in Him] shall change and renew their strength and power; they shall lift their wings and mount up [close to God] as eagles [mount up to the sun]; they shall run and not be weary, they shall walk and not faint or become tired.

Isaiah 40:28-31

Bless (affectionately, gratefully praise) the Lord, O my soul; and all that is [deepest] within me, bless His holy name! Bless (affectionately, gratefully praise) the Lord, O my soul, and forget not [one of] all His benefits —

Who forgives [every one of] all your iniquities, Who heals [each one of] all your diseases,

Who redeems your life from the pit and corruption, Who beautifies, dignifies, and crowns you with loving-kindness and tender mercy;

Who satisfies your mouth [your necessity and desire at your personal age and situation] with good so that your youth, renewed, is like the eagle's [strong, overcoming, soaring]!

Psalm 103:1-5

Once again, know that you are not alone. The Lord is with you. He understands what you are going through and has promised to be with you in every trial of life. When you "feel" the loneliest and the most forsaken, open your mouth in faith and say emphatically, "I am *not* alone, for God is with me!"

While you are waiting for your healing to manifest, confess this out loud: "The healing power of God is working in me right now."

Also, read and confess these Scripture verses which assure you of the Lord's presence and power:

> But take notice, the hour is coming, and it has arrived, when you will all be dispersed and scattered, every man to his own home, leaving Me alone. Yet *I am not alone, because the Father is with Me.*
>
> I have told you these things, so that in Me you may have [perfect] peace and confidence. In the world you have tribulation and trials and distress and frustration; but be of good cheer [take courage; be confident, certain, undaunted]! For I have overcome the world. *[I have deprived it of power to harm you and have conquered it for you.]*

John 16:32,33

2. *"Press aggressively"* into a new life.

Not everything in your life is over; just one part of it has ended. One season has passed; another can now begin — if you are willing to take action.

Don't just passively sit and wait for something to happen or someone to come along. Pray — and then step out in faith.

Earlier I shared with you about my aunt and how difficult it was for her to begin a new life after the death of my uncle. However, as hard as that transition was, she made it. Now she travels with my husband and me and helps in our ministry to others. In our meetings, she sells cassette tapes of our seminars. At home, she cooks for us and, when she can, she babysits our grandchildren.

All of these things are a tremendous benefit to us and to the Kingdom of God. She has "pressed aggressively" into a new lifestyle and, in the process, has become a blessing to many.

If you are lonely, don't just sit and wish you would meet others. *Go make new friends!* Find someone else who is lonely too — someone even lonelier than you are — and be a friend to that individual. You will reap what you sow. God will return that friendship to you, multiplied many times over.

Our daughter Sandra went through a lonely time in her young adult years. It seemed that most of her friends had either gone off to college or got married, so she was spending a lot of lonely evenings at home.

Instead of sitting and feeling sorry for herself, she started "pressing aggressively" forward and going places on her own. She would attend church functions alone or go to a singles group at another church by herself. It was not easy for her, but she knew she had to do something besides just sit and wish for companionship.

You may say, "Well, Joyce, I'm not wishing, I'm believing." But I would remind you that the Bible teaches us that faith moves us to take God-inspired action. (James 2:17.) I am not suggesting works of the flesh, or just fleshly zeal, but I am saying to be bold and step out as God leads.

Sandra is now married to Steve, a young man she met at a function she attended alone. Her "corresponding actions" gave her faith a direction and a goal.

In the same way, put "hands and feet" to your prayers. Let your loneliness give birth to compassion within you for other lonely people and then *decide to do something about it!*

Read and meditate on the Scripture passages in the following section, allowing the Lord to speak through them to you in your present situation.

Part 2

Scriptures

Scriptures
To Overcome Loneliness and Grief

❧

God Is Always With You

...He [God] Himself has said, I will not in any way fail you nor give you up nor leave you without support. [I will] not, [I will] not, [I will] not in any degree leave you helpless nor forsake nor let [you] down (relax My hold on you)! [Assuredly not!]

Hebrews 13:5

...I will never leave thee, nor forsake thee.

Hebrews 13:5 KJV

Because he has set his love upon Me...I will never forsake him, no, never....

He shall call upon Me, and I will answer him; I will be with him in trouble, I will deliver him and honor him....

Psalm 91:14,15

You Cannot Be Separated From God's Love

Who shall ever separate us from Christ's love?...

For I am persuaded beyond doubt (am sure) that neither death nor life, nor angels nor principalities, nor things impending and threatening nor things to come, nor powers,

Nor height nor depth, nor anything else in all creation will be able to separate us from the love of God which is in Christ Jesus our Lord.

Romans 8:35,38,39

The Lord Will Take Care of You

The Lord is my Shepherd [to feed, guide, and shield me], I shall not lack.

Psalm 23:1

A father of the fatherless and a judge and protector of the widows is God in His holy habitation.

God places the solitary in families and gives the desolate a home in which to dwell; He leads the prisoners out to prosperity; but the rebellious dwell in a parched land.

Psalm 68:5,6

Although my father and my mother have forsaken me, yet the Lord will take me up [adopt me as His child].

Psalm 27:10

Fear not, for you shall not be ashamed; neither be confounded and depressed, for you shall not be put to shame. For you shall forget the shame of your youth, and you shall not [seriously] remember the reproach of your widowhood any more.

For your Maker is your Husband — the Lord of hosts is His name — and the Holy One of Israel is your Redeemer; the God of the whole earth He is called.

Isaiah 54:4,5

God Will Do a New Thing

Do not [earnestly] remember the former things; neither consider the things of old.

Behold, I am doing a new thing! Now it springs forth; do you not perceive and know it and will you not give heed to it? I will even make a way in the wilderness and rivers in the desert.

Isaiah 43:18,19

Behold, the former things have come to pass, and new things I now declare; before they spring forth I tell you of them.

Isaiah 42:9

Press On

I do not consider, brethren, that I have captured and made it my own [yet]; but one thing I do [it is my one aspiration]: forgetting what lies behind and straining forward to what lies ahead,

I press on toward the goal to win the [supreme and heavenly] prize to which God in Christ Jesus is calling us upward.

Philippians 3:13,14

Don't give up, give out or give in. Instead, press on — aggressively.

God Is Not Finished With You!

For I know the thoughts and plans that I have for you, says the Lord,

thoughts and plans for welfare and
peace and not for evil, to give you
hope in your final outcome.

Jeremiah 29:11

Conclusion

❧

Press aggressively forward into the next season of your life. Things may never be the way they used to be, but don't miss the rest of your life by living in the past.

The time has come to stop thinking and talking about the past. You have a future. The Holy Spirit is standing by ready to help you, comfort you and assist you in pressing on to fulfill God's marvelous plan for you.

Remember: God is not finished with you!

Endings Always Offer New Beginnings

In John 10:10, Jesus said, "The thief comes only in order to steal and kill and destroy. I came that they may have and enjoy life, and have it in abundance (to the full, till it overflows)."

No matter how good or how bad your life before your loss was, you cannot live in the past and enjoy life in the present and the future.

Whatever you have lost, be determined not to miss what remains.

Remember:

God is good.

He loves you very much.

He has a good plan for your life.

Prayer and Blessing

Now I want to pray for you and leave you with a final word of encouragement:

Father, I come to You in Jesus' name, presenting unto You all that He is and asking for Your grace and mercy.

This precious person for whom I am praying is hurting. I ask for the comfort of the Holy Spirit to flow to this individual beginning right now. Your Word says that You are the Healer of the brokenhearted. You have promised to bind up our wounds and heal our bruises.

We look to You, Lord, for truly You are our Helper in time of need. You have promised to place the solitary, the lonely, in families. I ask You, Lord, to do according to Your Word and give this child of Yours friends and family who will care for him or her.

Assist this person, Holy Spirit, as he or she takes steps of faith to build a new life. I ask You to prosper this individual mentally, physically, spiritually, financially and socially. Amen.

Child of God, I believe that the anointing of the Holy Spirit is flowing into you right now. I recommend that you remain in His presence for a period of time, allowing Him to minister to you. Let Him take the Word that I have shared with you and, as you wait, trust Him to work it in you.

I believe that a fresh wind of the Spirit is blowing on you to prepare you for a new season in your life. May the love of God, the grace of our Lord Jesus Christ and the communion of the Holy Spirit be with you.*

---

*Joyce recommends that you obtain her music and Scripture tape entitled "Healing the Brokenhearted." This special tape has helped thousands experience the healing power of God in their emotions, and Joyce believes it will also help you. In addition Joyce recommends a second music and Scripture tape entitled "Be Strong and Take Courage."(To purchase a copy of these tapes, call Life In The Word at 1-800-727-Word or write to Joyce at the address given in the back of this book).

Prayer
for a Personal Relationship
With the Lord

Jesus wants to save you and fill you with the Holy Spirit more than anything. If you have never invited Jesus, the Prince of Peace, to be your Lord and Savior, I invite you to do so now. Pray the following prayer, and if you are really sincere about it, you will experience a new life in Christ.

Father,

You loved the world so much, You gave Your only begotten Son to die for our sins so that whoever believes in Him will not perish, but have eternal life.

Your Word says we are saved by grace through faith as a gift from You. There is nothing we can do to earn salvation.

I believe and confess with my mouth that Jesus Christ is Your Son, the Savior of the world. I believe He died on the cross for me and bore all of my sins, paying the price for them. I believe in my heart that You raised Jesus from the dead.

I ask You to forgive my sins. I confess Jesus as my Lord. According to Your Word, I am saved and will spend eternity with You! Thank You, Father. I am so grateful! In Jesus' name, amen.

See John 3:16; Ephesians 2:8,9; Romans 10:9,10; 1 Corinthians 15:3,4; 1 John 1:9; 4:14-16; 5:1,12,13.

Endnotes

Chapter 2

1. Webster's II New Riverside University Dictionary, s.v. "lone."
2. Webster, s.v. "lonely."
3. Webster, s.v. "lonesome."
4. Webster, s.v. "alone."
5. Webster, s.v. "grief."
6. Webster, s.v. "grieve."
7. Based on Webster, s.v. "depression."

About the Author

❧

Joyce Meyer has been teaching the Word of God since 1976 and in full-time ministry since 1980. As an associate pastor at Life Christian Center in St. Louis, Missouri, she developed, coordinated and taught a weekly meeting known as "Life In The Word." After more than five years, the Lord brought it to a conclusion, directing her to establish her own ministry and call it "Life In The Word, Inc."

Joyce's "Life In The Word" radio broadcast is heard on over 250 stations nationwide. Joyce's 30-minute "Life In The Word With Joyce Meyer" television program was released in 1993 and is broadcast throughout the United States and several foreign countries. Her teaching tapes are enjoyed internationally. She travels extensively conducting Life In The Word conferences, as well as speaking in local churches.

Joyce and her husband, Dave, business administrator at Life In The Word, have been married for 31 years and are the parents of four children. Three are married, and their youngest son resides with them in Fenton, Missouri, a St. Louis suburb.

Joyce believes the call on her life is to establish believers in God's Word. She says, "Jesus died to set the captives free, and far too many Christians have little or no victory in their daily lives." Finding herself in the same situation many years ago, and having found freedom to live in victory through applying God's Word, Joyce goes equipped to set captives free and to exchange *ashes for beauty*.

Joyce has taught on emotional healing and related subjects in meetings all over the country, helping multiplied thousands. She has recorded over 175 different audio cassette albums and is the author of 30 books to help the Body of Christ on various topics.

Her "Emotional Healing Package" contains over 23 hours of teaching on the subject. Albums included in this package are: "Confidence"; "Beauty for Ashes" (includes a syllabus); "Managing Your Emotions"; "Bitterness, Resentment, and Unforgiveness"; "Root of Rejection"; and a 90-minute Scripture/music tape entitled, "Healing the Brokenhearted."

Joyce's "Mind Package" features five different audio tape series on the subject of the mind. They include: "Mental Strongholds and Mindsets"; "Wilderness Mentality"; "The Mind of the Flesh"; "The Wandering, Wondering Mind"; and "Mind, Mouth, Moods & Attitudes." The package also contains Joyce's powerful 260-page book, *Battlefield of the Mind.* On the subject of love she has two tape series entitled, "Love Is..." and "Love: The Ultimate Power."

Write to Joyce Meyer's office for a resource catalog and further information on

To contact the author write:

Joyce Meyer
Life In The Word, Inc.
P. O. Box 655
Fenton, Missouri 63026
or call:
(314) 349-0303

*Please include your testimony
or help received from this
book when you write.
Your prayer requests are welcome.*

In Canada, please write:
Joyce Meyer Ministries Canada, Inc.
P. O. Box 2995
London, ON N6A 4H9

In Australia, please write:
Joyce Meyer Ministries-Australia
Locked Bag 77
Mansfield Delivery Centre
Queensland 4122
or call:
(07) 3349 1200

Books by Joyce Meyer

Weary Warriors,
Fainting Saints

Life in the Word Devotional

Be Anxious for Nothing —
The Art of Casting Your Cares and Resting in God

The *Help Me!* Series:
I'm Alone!
I'm Stressed!
I'm Insecure!
I'm Discouraged!
I'm Depressed!
I'm Worried!
I'm Afraid!

Don't Dread —
Overcoming the Spirit of Dread
With the Supernatural Power of God

Managing Your Emotions
Instead of Your Emotions Managing You

Life in the Word

Healing the Brokenhearted

"Me and My Big Mouth!"

Prepare To Prosper

Do It! Afraid

*Expect a Move of God in Your Life...**Suddenly***

Available from your local bookstore.

Harrison House
Tulsa, Oklahoma 74153

The Harrison House Vision

Proclaiming the truth and the power
Of the Gospel of Jesus Christ
With excellence;

Challenging Christians to
Live victoriously,
Grow spiritually,
Know God intimately.